PSYCHODRAMA FOR HEALING

Transformative Techniques For Trauma Recovery, Emotional Release, And Personal Growth

DR. MELISSA STOTLER

Copyright © 2023 by Dr. Melissa Stotler

Disclaimer:

The data in this book, is solely meant to be informative and instructional.

This book is not intended to replace expert medical advice, diagnosis, or care. No medical, health, or other professional services are offered by the author, publisher, or any affiliated parties

Individual outcomes may differ in the practice of these therapies, which entail a variety of approaches and methodologies.

A one-on-one session with a trained or certified healthcare professional is still preferable. It is best to consult a trained healthcare provider before making any decisions regarding your health.

The author of this book is not affiliated with any specific website, product, or organization related to any of these therapies.

All reasonable measures have been taken by the author and publisher to guarantee the authenticity and dependability of the material contained in this book.

Contents

Psychodrama offers a transformative approach to healing, inviting individuals to explore their inner worlds and external relationships through dramatic enactment.

This book serves as a comprehensive guide to understanding and applying psychodrama, beginning with an exploration of its foundational elements.

The historical evolution and core principles of psychodrama provide a crucial context for its application, revealing how its techniques like role reversal and spontaneous drama can unlock deep-seated emotions and foster personal growth.

The preparation for a psychodrama session is meticulously detailed, emphasizing the importance of creating a safe and supportive environment. Clear objectives, relevant themes, and thorough participant preparation are essential for a successful session. This preparation ensures that every participant is well-equipped to engage deeply and meaningfully in the psychodramatic process.

The techniques of psychodrama are richly illustrated, focusing on role reversal, mirroring, spontaneity, and doubling.

These methods are instrumental in enhancing self-awareness, empathy, and emotional expression.

Additionally, the session structure and the role of the director are explored, highlighting how to effectively engage participants and manage group dynamics to facilitate a productive therapeutic experience.

Real-life applications of psychodrama are examined through compelling case studies and success stories, demonstrating its efficacy in various therapeutic settings.

Advanced techniques, such as sociometric mapping and future projection, are also discussed, offering insights into how psychodrama can be adapted for complex issues and integrated with other therapeutic approaches.

Ethical considerations are a cornerstone of the practice, covering essential aspects such as confidentiality, informed consent, and cultural sensitivity. Addressing common concerns, including managing resistance and emotional overwhelm, ensures that practitioners are well-prepared to navigate the challenges that may arise during sessions.

This book also addresses frequently asked questions, guides on finding qualified psychodrama therapists, and offers resources for further learning and professional development.

Through its detailed exploration of psychodrama, this book stands as a vital resource for practitioners and individuals seeking to harness the power of dramatic enactment for healing and personal growth.

CHAPTER ONE

THE BASICS OF PSYCHODRAMA

Historical Background: Origins And Evolution Of Psychodrama

Psychodrama, a therapeutic method developed in the early 20th century, traces its roots back to the pioneering work of Jacob L.

Moreno. Moreno, a Romanian psychiatrist and psychologist, is credited with founding this innovative approach.

 His early experiments in group therapy, which involved using spontaneous drama and role-playing to explore emotional and psychological issues, laid the foundation for psychodrama.

Initially, Moreno's ideas were considered unconventional. However, his work quickly gained recognition for its unique approach to psychotherapy, emphasizing the use of action and dramatic techniques. Over the decades, psychodrama evolved from Moreno's initial concepts into a structured therapeutic modality with well-defined techniques and procedures. Today, it is used globally by therapists to address a wide range of psychological issues, blending creativity with traditional therapeutic practices.

Core Principles: Key Theories And Concepts

Psychodrama is built upon several core principles that guide its practice. At its heart is the concept of spontaneity and creativity. Moreno believed that these elements are crucial for personal growth and healing. By engaging in spontaneous actions and role-playing, individuals can access and express emotions that might be difficult to articulate in conventional therapy.

Another key principle is the idea of "tele," or the emotional bond between people. Psychodrama emphasizes understanding and altering these emotional connections to facilitate healing. Through role reversal and other techniques, participants can explore and transform their relationships and emotional patterns.

The therapeutic process in psychodrama is also grounded in the concept of the "here and now." This focus on the present moment allows individuals to experience and process emotions in real time, enhancing the effectiveness of the therapeutic work. The use of drama and role-play in this context helps to externalize and make sense of internal conflicts and issues.

Main Techniques: Techniques Such As Role Reversal And Spontaneous Drama

Psychodrama employs various techniques to facilitate therapeutic progress. One of the most fundamental techniques is role reversal. This involves participants switching roles with others in their lives or with aspects of themselves. By embodying another person's perspective, individuals gain insight into their feelings and behaviors, which can lead to greater empathy and understanding.

Another key technique is spontaneous drama, where participants act out scenes from their lives or imaginary scenarios. This method helps individuals explore emotions and situations dynamically and interactively. Spontaneous drama encourages creativity and allows participants to experiment with different ways of handling their issues.

The protagonist is another central element in psychodrama.

This person is the main focus of the session, exploring their issues through role-playing and dramatic enactments. 4

The protagonist's experiences are often brought to life with the help of auxiliary egos, who represent significant people in the protagonist's life or various aspects of the protagonist's psyche.

Setting Up A Session: Essential Components Of A Psychodrama Session

Setting up a psychodrama session involves several essential components to ensure its effectiveness.

Preparation is crucial, including setting up a safe and comfortable environment where participants feel secure to express themselves freely. The physical space should be conducive to movement and role-playing, with enough room for participants to act out scenes.

The director plays a pivotal role in guiding the session. This person facilitates the process, ensuring that the techniques are used appropriately and that the session remains focused and productive. The director also helps participants stay engaged and manage the emotional intensity that can arise during psychodramatic work.

The warm-up phase is another important aspect of session preparation. This phase helps participants transition into the psychodramatic mode, easing them into the work with activities or exercises that build trust and prepare them emotionally and mentally for the session.

Finally, debriefing is an essential component at the end of the session. This phase allows participants to process their experiences, discuss insights gained, and integrate the emotions and revelations from the session into their everyday lives.

Roles And Responsibilities: Understanding The Roles Of The Director, Protagonist, And Auxiliary Egos

In a psychodrama session, understanding the roles and responsibilities of each participant is crucial for a successful therapeutic experience.

The director is responsible for orchestrating the session. This role involves creating a safe and supportive environment, guiding the therapeutic process, and helping participants navigate their emotional experiences.

The director also ensures that the techniques are used effectively and that the session adheres to the therapeutic goals.

The protagonist is the central figure in the psychodrama. This individual focuses on their issues and uses role-playing to explore and resolve them.

The protagonist's active engagement in the process is essential, as their willingness to delve into their experiences and emotions drives the session's progress.

Auxiliary egos are participants who take on roles that represent other people or aspects of the protagonist's life. These individuals help to bring the protagonist's inner world to life by acting out scenes and interactions.

Auxiliary egos provide crucial support by embodying different perspectives and facilitating the exploration of relationships and emotions.

Each role in psychodrama is interdependent, with the director, protagonist, and auxiliary egos working together to achieve therapeutic goals and promote healing through dynamic and interactive processes.

CHAPTER TWO

PREPARING FOR PSYCHODRAMA

Creating A Safe Space: How To Establish A Supportive Environment

Creating a safe space is essential for a successful psychodrama session. Start by ensuring the physical environment is comfortable and free from distractions. Choose a quiet, well-lit room where participants feel at ease. Arrange seating in a way that encourages openness and minimizes barriers between participants. Use soft lighting and calming colors to foster a relaxed atmosphere.

Establish ground rules to promote respect and confidentiality. Communicate these rules at the beginning of the session to ensure everyone understands and agrees. Encourage participants to express their feelings and thoughts openly without fear of judgment. As the facilitator, model empathy and active listening to create an atmosphere of trust and safety.

Identifying Goals: Setting Clear Objectives For The Session

Setting clear objectives is crucial for directing the focus of the psychodrama session. Begin by discussing with participants what they hope to achieve. Goals should be specific, measurable, and relevant to the participants' needs. For example, a goal might be to explore unresolved feelings about a past event or to practice new coping strategies in a controlled setting.

Ensure that goals are realistic and attainable within the session's timeframe. Break down larger objectives into smaller, manageable steps to make progress easier to track. Regularly revisit and adjust these goals as needed based on the participants' feedback and the session's progress.

Selecting Themes: Choosing Relevant And Meaningful Themes To Explore

Choosing the right themes is key to a productive psychodrama session. Themes should be relevant to the participants' current issues or concerns. Engage with participants to identify themes that resonate with their personal experiences or goals. Common themes might include relationship dynamics, self-esteem issues, or coping with trauma.

Once a theme is selected, tailor it to fit the specific needs of the group. Incorporate elements that will engage participants and encourage them to explore the theme deeply. This might involve using scenarios or role-playing that reflect real-life situations related to the theme. Ensure the theme is broad enough to allow for exploration but focused enough to guide the session effectively.

Preparing Participants: Guidelines For Preparing Individuals For Their Role In The Session

Preparation is key for participants to fully engage in psychodrama. Begin by explaining the format and purpose of the session.

Discuss the roles they may play and the scenarios they might encounter. Provide clear instructions on what is expected from them during the session.

Encourage participants to reflect on their personal experiences related to the theme. They might benefit from journaling or discussing their thoughts with a trusted friend or therapist beforehand.

It's also helpful to conduct a brief warm-up exercise to help participants relax and become comfortable with the process. Ensure that everyone understands their role and feels ready to participate before the session begins.

Logistics And Materials: Necessary Materials And Session Logistics

Proper logistics and materials are essential for a smooth psychodrama session. Prepare any materials needed, such as props, costumes, or visual aids that can help bring the scenarios to life. Make sure these materials are relevant to the theme and accessible to all participants.

Plan the session's structure, including the sequence of activities and time allocation. Ensure that there is enough time for each activity and for debriefing afterward.

Consider having a plan for unexpected issues, such as technical difficulties or emotional responses.

Set up the room in advance, arranging furniture and materials to facilitate movement and interaction. Have a schedule or agenda to keep the session on track. Ensure that there are adequate resources available, such as refreshments or breaks, to maintain participants' comfort and engagement throughout the session.

CHAPTER THREE

PSYCHODRAMA TECHNIQUES

Role Reversal: Understanding And Applying This Core Technique

Role reversal is a foundational technique in psychodrama that allows participants to step into the shoes of another person, often someone significant in their lives.

This technique involves the participant switching roles with someone else in a dramatic scene, thus experiencing the situation from a different perspective.

To apply role reversal effectively, the therapist first guides the participant to identify and articulate their role and the role of the other person they wish to explore.

This might involve a family member, a colleague, or any individual with whom they have unresolved issues. The participant then physically and emotionally switches roles, speaking and behaving as if they are the other person.

This process helps in gaining new insights and understanding the feelings, motivations, and reactions of the other individual.

The power of role reversal lies in its ability to foster empathy and self-awareness. By seeing and feeling things from another's viewpoint, participants can often resolve conflicts, alleviate misunderstandings, and develop a deeper emotional connection with others.

To maximize the benefits of role reversal, ensure that participants are comfortable and prepared for this deep dive into their emotional landscape.

Mirroring: Using Mirroring To Enhance Self-Awareness And Empathy

Mirroring is a technique in psychodrama where one participant replicates the actions, emotions, and expressions of another participant or the protagonist in a scene. This technique is used to enhance self-awareness and build empathy by reflecting on what is being expressed, both verbally and non-verbally.

In a typical mirroring exercise, a participant or group member observes the protagonist's behavior and then mirrors it as closely as possible. This includes repeating their movements, speech patterns, and emotional expressions. The therapist may also use mirroring to help the protagonist become more aware of their own behavior and emotional state.

Mirroring serves several purposes: it helps participants recognize and understand their own emotions more clearly, provides insight into how others perceive them, and fosters a sense of connection and validation. When participants see their behaviors and emotions reflected in them, they can often gain new perspectives and insights that contribute to their personal growth and emotional healing.

Spontaneity And Creativity: Encouraging Spontaneous Expression And Creative Solutions

Spontaneity and creativity are essential elements in psychodrama, aimed at breaking away from rigid thought patterns and encouraging free expression. These techniques are used to foster an environment where participants feel safe to explore and express their true feelings without self-censorship.

To encourage spontaneity, therapists create a supportive atmosphere where participants are invited to act out their thoughts and emotions in the moment. This might involve improvisational exercises, free association, or unplanned role plays.

The focus is on allowing participants to react and respond in real time, which can lead to unexpected insights and breakthroughs.

Creativity in psychodrama can also involve using props, music, or artistic elements to stimulate imaginative expression.

By engaging in creative activities, participants often discover new ways to approach their problems, find innovative solutions, and express emotions that might be difficult to articulate through words alone. The key is to provide a space where participants feel liberated to experiment and explore without fear of judgment.

Doubling: Utilizing Doubling To Support Participants In Expressing Hidden Emotions

Doubling is a technique where a participant, known as the "doubling" person, stands beside the protagonist and expresses thoughts or feelings that the protagonist might be struggling to voice. This technique helps to uncover and articulate hidden emotions and internal conflicts.

In a doubling exercise, the therapist identifies moments when the protagonist appears to be holding back or struggling with their emotions. The doubling person then voices these unspoken thoughts or feelings, often reflecting the protagonist's internal struggles.

 This externalization can help the protagonist feel understood and supported, as well as provide a clearer understanding of their own emotions.

Doubling can be particularly useful for exploring complex or repressed feelings that the protagonist might find difficult to confront on their own.

By having these emotions voiced by someone else, participants can more readily engage with them, work through them, and integrate them into their overall emotional experience.

This technique fosters a sense of safety and validation, making it easier for participants to address and resolve their internal conflicts.

Playback: Reviewing and Reflecting on the Enacted Scenes

Playback is a technique used in psychodrama to review and reflect on the scenes that have been enacted during a session.

This involves replaying significant moments or entire scenes to gain deeper insights and understanding of the experience.

During playback, the therapist and participants revisit the dramatized scenes, often with the help of other group members who reenact key moments.

This review process allows participants to observe and reflect on their actions, emotions, and interactions from a new perspective. It provides an opportunity to analyze what occurred, how it felt, and what insights can be gained.

Playback helps participants process and integrate their experiences by reinforcing learning, clarifying misunderstandings, and providing a chance to rehearse new responses. This technique not only deepens the therapeutic work but also enhances the overall effectiveness of the psychodrama process, as participants can see how their actions impact themselves and others.

CHAPTER FOUR

CONDUCTING A PSYCHODRAMA SESSION

Session Structure: Typical Flow Of A Psychodrama Session

A psychodrama session typically follows a structured flow designed to help participants explore and resolve personal issues through role-playing and dramatic techniques. The session often begins with a warm-up activity, which helps participants become comfortable and attuned to the group dynamic. This initial phase is crucial for setting the tone and encouraging openness.

Following the warm-up, the session moves into the main action phase, where the protagonist—the person whose issue is being explored—chooses a scene or situation to dramatize. This is usually followed by the development of the scene, where participants assume roles and act out the chosen scenario. The director, or facilitator, guides this process, ensuring that the scene unfolds in a way that is both therapeutic and insightful.

The session concludes with a sharing and reflection phase. Participants discuss their experiences, insights gained, and any emotional reactions they had during the dramatization. This debriefing helps solidify the therapeutic benefits of the session and provides closure for both the protagonist and the group.

Role Of The Director: Leading And Guiding The Session

The director plays a pivotal role in a psychodrama session, acting as the facilitator who guides the entire process. This involves setting the stage for the session, introducing the main themes or issues, and ensuring that the group adheres to the psychodramatic techniques.

One of the primary responsibilities of the director is to establish a safe and supportive environment. This includes setting clear boundaries and rules, encouraging trust among participants, and being attentive to the emotional needs of individuals. The director also helps the protagonist articulate their concerns and select scenes that will be most beneficial for their therapeutic goals.

During the action phase, the director provides direction and feedback, helping participants stay engaged and focused. They intervene when necessary to guide the drama or address any issues that arise. The director's role is crucial in maintaining the flow of the session and ensuring that the dramatic process remains therapeutic and constructive.

Engaging Participants: Techniques To Encourage Active Participation

Engaging participants in a psychodrama session is essential for maximizing the therapeutic impact. Various techniques can be employed to encourage active participation and ensure that everyone feels involved.

One effective technique is to use warm-up exercises that help participants become more comfortable and relaxed. These activities can include group games, role-reversal exercises, or creative expression tasks that build group cohesion and reduce anxiety.

Another technique is to encourage role-taking and improvisation. Allowing participants to step into different roles and explore various perspectives can deepen their engagement and enhance their understanding of the issues at hand. Providing clear instructions and setting up scenarios that resonate with participants' personal experiences can also boost their involvement.

Regularly checking in with participants and soliciting their feedback can help maintain their engagement. Encouraging open communication and validating their contributions ensures that everyone feels valued and invested in the session.

Managing Group Dynamics: Handling Interactions And Conflicts Within The Group

Managing group dynamics is a critical aspect of conducting a successful psychodrama session. Group interactions can vary widely, and conflicts or challenging dynamics may arise that need to be addressed promptly and effectively.

One key strategy for managing group dynamics is to establish clear ground rules at the beginning of the session. These rules should outline expected behaviors, confidentiality, and respect for others, helping to create a safe space for all participants.

When conflicts or tensions arise, the director should address them calmly and constructively. This might involve facilitating a discussion between conflicting parties, providing support to those who are feeling overwhelmed or adjusting the session's focus to better meet the needs of the group.

It's also important to recognize and address any power imbalances or dominance issues within the group. Ensuring that everyone has an opportunity to participate and express their views can help maintain a balanced and supportive environment.

Closing The Session: Effective Ways To Conclude And Debrief The Session

Closing a psychodrama session effectively is crucial for ensuring that participants leave with a sense of completion and understanding.

The closing phase typically involves debriefing and reflection, which helps participants integrate their experiences and insights from the session.

One effective way to conclude a session is to facilitate a group discussion where participants can share their feelings, observations, and takeaways. This discussion allows individuals to process their experiences, gain feedback from others, and consolidate the therapeutic benefits of the session.

Another important aspect of closing is to provide individual feedback to the protagonist and other participants.

This feedback should be constructive and supportive, helping individuals recognize their progress and areas for further exploration.

Finally, it's essential to end the session on a positive note, reinforcing the group's sense of accomplishment and readiness for future sessions.

This can be achieved through a closing activity, a summary of key insights, or expressions of appreciation for each participant's contributions.

CHAPTER FIVE

CASE STUDIES AND EXAMPLES

Real-Life Applications: Examples Of Psychodrama Used In Various Therapeutic Settings

Psychodrama, a therapeutic technique developed by Jacob Moreno, has found its way into diverse settings, each demonstrating its adaptability and effectiveness. In a clinical setting, psychodrama has been used to treat individuals with trauma-related disorders. For instance, in a case involving a survivor of abuse, psychodrama facilitated the person's exploration of past experiences by re-enacting significant moments. This process allowed the individual to express and process emotions in a controlled environment, leading to improved emotional regulation and insight.

In community mental health centers, psychodrama is utilized in group therapy sessions. A notable example is a support group for individuals with anxiety disorders. Through role-playing and spontaneous drama, participants confront their fears and practice coping strategies in a supportive setting. This method not only helps individuals gain new perspectives on their issues but also fosters a sense of solidarity and mutual understanding among group members.

Educational settings have also benefited from psychodrama. For example, in a school counseling program, psychodrama was employed to help students with social skills deficits. By acting out social scenarios and receiving feedback, students improved their interpersonal skills and built confidence in navigating social interactions.

Success Stories: Case Studies Highlighting Successful Outcomes

Several case studies illustrate the profound impact psychodrama can have. One success story involves a patient dealing with chronic depression. Through psychodrama, the patient was able to re-enact pivotal moments from their past, gaining insight into unresolved issues. This process was instrumental in helping the patient confront and reframe negative beliefs, leading to a significant reduction in depressive symptoms.

Another compelling case involved a group of veterans with PTSD. In group psychodrama sessions, veterans took on roles representing their experiences and emotions. This approach not only provided a safe space to express difficult feelings but also helped participants connect with others who had similar experiences. The outcome was a notable improvement in their coping mechanisms and a stronger sense of community.

A third example is a teenager struggling with identity issues. Through psychodrama, the teen was able to explore different aspects of their identity by taking on various roles. This exploration led to greater self-acceptance and clarity about their personal goals and values.

Challenges And Solutions: Common Challenges Faced And Strategies To Overcome Them

Despite its benefits, psychodrama comes with its own set of challenges. One common challenge is resistance from participants. Individuals may initially be hesitant to engage in role-playing or confront uncomfortable emotions. To address this, therapists often employ gradual exposure techniques, starting with less intense scenarios and building up to more significant issues as trust and comfort grow.

Another challenge is managing group dynamics. In group settings, conflicts or dominant personalities can disrupt the therapeutic process.

Effective facilitation is key here. Therapists need to establish clear group norms and actively manage dynamics to ensure that everyone's voice is heard and respected.

A logistical challenge is the need for adequate space and resources. Psychodrama often requires physical space for role-playing and access to various props.

Solutions include creative use of available resources and, when possible, preparing participants to use minimal props to facilitate their dramatizations.

Lessons Learned: Insights Gained From Different Cases

From various case studies, several valuable lessons emerge. One key insight is the importance of creating a safe and supportive environment. Participants need to feel secure in expressing their emotions and exploring their experiences.

Therapists play a crucial role in fostering this sense of safety through empathetic engagement and clear boundaries.

Another lesson is the adaptability of psychodrama to different therapeutic needs. Whether working with trauma, anxiety, or identity issues, psychodrama can be tailored to meet individual needs, making it a versatile tool in therapy. This flexibility underscores the importance of therapists being well-versed in the techniques and able to adjust their approach based on the specific context and goals of therapy.

Finally, the therapeutic relationship is crucial. Success in psychodrama often hinges on the strength of the therapeutic alliance. Building trust and rapport with participants enhances their willingness to engage in the process and maximizes the therapeutic benefits.

Application To Different Issues: Adapting Psychodrama For Diverse Psychological Concerns

Psychodrama's versatility allows it to be adapted for a wide range of psychological concerns. For example, in treating trauma, psychodrama techniques such as role reversal and doubling can help individuals process traumatic memories and gain new perspectives. By re-enacting traumatic events from different viewpoints, participants can integrate their experiences and reduce the emotional charge associated with them.

In addressing anxiety disorders, psychodrama can be used to simulate anxiety-provoking situations in a controlled setting.

Participants can practice coping strategies and build resilience by facing their fears in a supportive environment.

This experiential approach can be particularly effective in helping individuals develop practical skills for managing anxiety in real-life situations.

For issues related to self-esteem and identity, psychodrama allows individuals to explore different facets of their identity and personal history.

Through role-playing and improvisation, participants can gain insight into their self-concept and develop a more positive self-image.

Psychodrama's ability to address a wide array of psychological concerns makes it a valuable therapeutic tool. Its adaptability ensures that it can be tailored to meet the specific needs of individuals and groups, facilitating healing and growth across various contexts.

CHAPTER SIX

ADVANCED PSYCHODRAMA TECHNIQUES

Advanced Role Reversal: Deepening The Technique For Complex Issues

Role reversal is a cornerstone of psychodrama, allowing individuals to step into the shoes of others to gain insight and empathy.

To deepen this technique for addressing complex issues, advanced role reversal involves a more nuanced approach.

Instead of merely swapping roles, participants engage in multi-layered role reversals where they may switch between multiple perspectives in a single session.

This technique often requires careful facilitation to manage emotional intensity and ensure that all perspectives are explored thoroughly.

For example, if a participant is struggling with a conflict between a parent and a partner, advanced role reversal might involve not only stepping into each person's shoes but also exploring the roles of secondary figures like friends or colleagues who may influence the situation.

The goal is to help participants understand the interplay of various viewpoints and emotions, leading to deeper insights and more effective resolutions. Facilitators may use guided imagery or written prompts to support participants in navigating these complex role reversals.

Sociometric Mapping: Exploring Relationships And Social Dynamics Within The Group

Sociometric mapping is a technique used to visualize and explore the social dynamics and relationships within a group. This process involves creating a visual representation of how individuals in a group perceive their connections to one another. Participants may be asked to place themselves on a chart based on their feelings of closeness, support, or conflict with other group members.

To conduct sociometric mapping, facilitators typically start by identifying key social dimensions relevant to the group, such as trust, influence, or conflict. Participants then use markers, stickers, or drawings to position themselves and others according to these dimensions. This map helps in understanding the underlying social dynamics and patterns within the group.

The insights gained from sociometric mapping can be used to address group cohesion issues, identify sources of tension, and enhance overall group functioning. Facilitators can use this information to tailor interventions and foster a more supportive and collaborative group environment.

Future Projection: Using Psychodrama To Explore Future Scenarios And Goals

Future projection in psychodrama is a technique used to help individuals visualize and plan for future scenarios and goals. This technique involves creating and enacting scenes that represent potential future outcomes or aspirations, allowing participants to explore their hopes, fears, and strategies for achieving their goals.

To implement future projections, facilitators guide participants in imagining a future scenario, such as a career milestone or a personal achievement. Participants then role-play various aspects of this future scenario, including potential challenges and resources. This approach helps individuals gain clarity on their goals, identify possible obstacles, and develop actionable plans.

Future projection can be particularly effective in goal-setting and career planning, as it allows individuals to experiment with different strategies and perspectives. By acting out future scenarios, participants can better understand their motivations and make more informed decisions about their paths forward.

Working with Complex Themes: Techniques for Addressing Difficult or Sensitive Topics

Addressing complex or sensitive themes in psychodrama requires specialized techniques to ensure that participants feel safe and supported while exploring challenging issues. This might involve using structured exercises to gently introduce and manage difficult topics.

One effective approach is to use a "sculpting" technique, where participants create physical representations of their feelings or situations using objects or other people as stand-ins. This can provide a tangible way to discuss and address complex issues without overwhelming participants.

Another technique involves using "protagonist" work, where a participant takes on the role of the central figure in a scenario involving a complex theme. This allows them to explore their feelings and reactions in a controlled environment, with the support of the group and facilitator.

Facilitators should be attentive to participants' emotional responses and use techniques such as debriefing or grounding exercises to help manage any distress that arises. Creating a supportive atmosphere is crucial for working with sensitive topics effectively.

Integrating Other Therapies: Combining Psychodrama With Other Therapeutic Approaches

Integrating psychodrama with other therapeutic approaches can enhance the effectiveness of treatment by combining different techniques to address a range of issues. For example, combining psychodrama with cognitive-behavioral therapy (CBT) can provide a holistic approach to addressing both the emotional and cognitive aspects of a problem.

In practice, this integration might involve using psychodramatic role-plays to explore emotional experiences and then applying CBT techniques to develop coping strategies and challenge negative thought patterns. Alternatively, integrating psychodrama with mindfulness practices can help participants stay grounded and present while engaging in intense emotional work.

Facilitators should carefully consider how different therapeutic approaches complement each other and ensure that the integration supports the participant's goals. Collaboration with other therapists or practitioners may also be beneficial to create a cohesive treatment plan that leverages the strengths of each approach.

CHAPTER SEVEN

ETHICAL CONSIDERATIONS

Confidentiality: Ensuring Privacy And Confidentiality In Sessions

In psychodrama, confidentiality is a cornerstone of the therapeutic process. Maintaining privacy ensures that participants feel safe and are more likely to engage openly in their healing journey. As a therapist, it's crucial to establish clear guidelines about confidentiality from the beginning of the therapy. This involves explaining to participants how their personal information will be protected and the limits of confidentiality, such as instances where there is a risk of harm to themselves or others.

During sessions, it's important to avoid discussing any details of the sessions outside of the therapeutic environment. This means that even casual conversations with colleagues or friends should be free from any specifics about what occurred during sessions. Additionally, when documenting sessions or sharing insights for supervision, care should be taken to anonymize any identifying information to protect the participant's identity. Upholding these practices not only fosters trust but also ensures that the therapeutic environment remains secure and supportive.

Informed Consent: The Importance Of Obtaining Consent From Participants

Informed consent is a fundamental ethical practice in psychodrama, involving providing participants with all necessary information about the therapy before they agree to participate. This process ensures that individuals understand the nature of psychodrama, the techniques used, potential risks, and their right to withdraw at any time.

Before starting therapy, you should clearly explain the goals, methods, and potential outcomes of psychodrama. Participants should be given ample opportunity to ask questions and express any concerns.

It's also important to outline how their participation will be recorded and used, including any potential use in educational or research contexts. Participants must sign a consent form that confirms they have understood and agreed to these terms. Regularly revisiting consent throughout the therapy process is also beneficial, as it reaffirms their ongoing agreement and provides space for any new concerns to be addressed.

Cultural Sensitivity: Adapting Techniques To Respect Cultural Differences

Cultural sensitivity in psychodrama involves recognizing and respecting the diverse backgrounds and values of participants. Adapting techniques to fit cultural contexts ensures that the therapy is both respectful and effective. This means understanding and integrating cultural norms, traditions, and values into the therapeutic process.

To practice cultural sensitivity, start by educating yourself about the cultural backgrounds of your participants. This includes being aware of their beliefs, traditions, and social norms. During sessions, be mindful of how cultural differences might impact their responses and experiences. For instance, certain techniques or role-playing scenarios might need to be adjusted to align with cultural sensitivities or preferences. Open communication about cultural considerations with participants can help in adapting methods appropriately and creating a supportive environment that honors their cultural identity.

Handling Emotional Distress: Addressing And Managing Intense Emotions

Handling emotional distress effectively is crucial in psychodrama, as participants may experience intense emotions during sessions. It's essential to approach these situations with empathy and skill, ensuring that participants feel supported and understood.

When a participant shows signs of emotional distress, it's important to acknowledge their feelings and provide a safe space for them to express themselves. Techniques such as grounding exercises or guided breathing can help manage acute distress. Additionally, providing reassurance and validating their emotions can foster a supportive environment. If the distress becomes overwhelming, it's appropriate to pause the session and address their needs, whether that means taking a break or shifting focus to a less intense aspect of the session. Offering follow-up support and resources for additional help outside of sessions can also be beneficial in helping participants navigate their emotions.

Professional Boundaries: Maintaining Appropriate Boundaries As A Therapist

Maintaining professional boundaries is vital in psychodrama to ensure a therapeutic relationship remains respectful and effective. Boundaries help define the roles and limits of the therapist-participant relationship, preventing any potential misuse of power or emotional entanglement.

As a therapist, establish clear and consistent boundaries from the start. This includes setting limits on personal disclosures, and ensuring that the focus remains on the participant's needs rather than the therapist's. Be mindful of the emotional and physical space between you and the participant, maintaining a professional demeanor throughout. Avoid engaging in any behavior that could be interpreted as favoritism or inappropriate, and handle any personal disclosures from participants with care, ensuring they do not affect the therapeutic process. Regularly reflecting on and discussing boundaries with supervisors or peers can help in maintaining appropriate practices and addressing any challenges that arise.

CHAPTER EIGHT

COMMON CONCERNS IN PSYCHODRAMA FOR HEALING

Managing Resistance: Strategies For Dealing With Participant Resistance

In psychodrama, resistance from participants can be a common challenge. Resistance often manifests as reluctance to engage, defensiveness, or avoidance of certain topics. Addressing these behaviors is crucial for the therapeutic process.

One effective strategy is to establish a strong therapeutic alliance. Building trust with participants can reduce resistance by creating a safe and supportive environment. Start by validating their feelings and experiences, which helps them feel heard and respected.

Additionally, it can be helpful to gently explore the source of resistance. Open-ended questions and reflective listening can uncover underlying fears or concerns.

For example, you might ask, "What is it about this role or scenario that feels uncomfortable for you?" Understanding these dynamics allows you to address specific issues and adjust your approach accordingly.

Gradual exposure can also be effective. Rather than pushing participants to confront challenging issues immediately, start with less intense scenarios and progressively increase the level of difficulty as they become more comfortable. This approach helps participants build confidence and reduces resistance over time.

Addressing Emotional Overwhelm: How To Handle Overwhelming Emotions During Sessions

Emotional overwhelm can arise during psychodrama sessions, especially when participants confront deeply personal or distressing material. It's essential to manage these emotions to ensure the session remains productive and safe.

First, create a supportive atmosphere by encouraging participants to express their emotions freely. Validate their feelings and reassure them that it is normal to experience intense emotions during the process. This acknowledgment helps participants feel supported rather than isolated in their experience.

Implement grounding techniques to help participants manage overwhelming emotions.

Techniques such as deep breathing, mindfulness, or physical grounding exercises (like holding onto a chair or touching a reassuring object) can help participants regain their composure and focus.

It's also important to have a plan for immediate emotional support. This might include taking a short break, offering one-on-one support, or providing access to additional counseling resources if needed. Encourage participants to communicate openly about their emotional state and to take breaks as necessary.

Dealing With Conflict: Techniques For Resolving Conflicts Within The Group

Conflicts within a psychodrama group can disrupt the therapeutic process and hinder participants' progress. Effectively addressing and resolving these conflicts is essential for maintaining a productive and harmonious environment.

Start by identifying the source of the conflict. This might involve discussing the issues openly with the group or having private conversations with the involved parties. Understanding the root cause of the conflict allows you to address it more effectively.

Facilitate open and respectful communication among participants. Encourage them to express their viewpoints and feelings without blame or judgment.

Techniques such as active listening and "I" statements (e.g., "I feel upset when...") can help participants communicate their needs and concerns constructively.

Mediation can also be a valuable tool for resolving conflicts. As the facilitator, guide the group through a structured mediation process where each party can present their perspective and work together to find a resolution. This approach promotes understanding and collaboration, helping to resolve conflicts in a way that benefits everyone involved.

Ensuring Participant Safety: Safeguarding Participants' Physical and Emotional Well-Being

Ensuring the safety of participants is a fundamental aspect of psychodrama. Both physical and emotional safety must be prioritized to create a secure environment for healing.

Begin by setting clear boundaries and guidelines for the session. Explain the rules of engagement, including respecting personal space and maintaining confidentiality. Ensure that participants understand and agree to these guidelines before starting the session.

Monitor participants closely for signs of distress or discomfort. If a participant exhibits signs of physical or emotional distress, intervene promptly to provide support. This might involve taking a break, offering one-on-one support, or adjusting the session's focus to address their needs.

It's also important to provide aftercare and follow-up support. Offer resources or referrals for additional counseling or support if participants need help processing their experiences after the session. Ensuring that participants have access to ongoing support contributes to their overall safety and well-being.

Evaluating Effectiveness: Assessing The Impact And Effectiveness Of Psychodrama Sessions

Evaluating the effectiveness of psychodrama sessions is crucial for understanding their impact and making necessary adjustments. Regular assessment helps ensure that the therapeutic process is meeting participants' needs and achieving desired outcomes.

Begin by soliciting feedback from participants. Use structured tools such as surveys or questionnaires to gather their insights about the session. Ask questions about what they found helpful, what challenges they encountered, and how they feel about their progress.

Additionally, observe changes in participants' behavior and attitudes over time. Look for improvements in their emotional expression, interpersonal relationships, or coping skills. Document these observations to track progress and identify areas for further development.

Regularly review the goals of the psychodrama sessions and assess whether they are being met. Reflect on the effectiveness of the techniques and interventions used and make adjustments as needed. Continuous evaluation helps refine the therapeutic process and enhances its overall effectiveness.

CHAPTER NINE

FAQS AND ADDITIONAL RESOURCES

Frequently Asked Questions: Common Questions And Answers About Psychodrama

What is psychodrama?

Psychodrama is a therapeutic technique that uses guided drama and role-playing to help individuals explore and resolve emotional conflicts.

It involves acting out scenarios from one's life or imagined situations to gain insight and achieve healing. This method can be performed individually or in groups and often incorporates elements such as improvisation and spontaneous expression.

How does psychodrama work?

In a psychodrama session, participants act out scenes from their lives, which may include past experiences, present dilemmas, or future aspirations.

This dramatization helps individuals externalize their feelings and thoughts, allowing them to view their problems from different perspectives.

A trained psychodrama therapist guides the process, helping participants gain clarity and understanding of their emotions and behaviors.

Who can benefit from psychodrama?

Psychodrama can be beneficial for a wide range of people, including those struggling with trauma, anxiety, depression, relationship issues, and self-esteem problems. It is also useful for individuals seeking personal growth or wishing to explore their inner conflicts in a supportive environment.

Is psychodrama safe?

Yes, psychodrama is generally considered safe when conducted by a qualified therapist. The process is designed to be supportive and non-threatening.

However, as with any therapeutic approach, it is important to work with a trained professional who can ensure that the process is conducted in a safe and respectful manner.

How long does a psychodrama session last?

A typical psychodrama session can last between 1.5 to 2 hours. Sessions may vary in length depending on the format (individual or group) and the specific needs of the participants. Longer workshops or intensive sessions may also be offered.

Finding A Psychodrama Therapist: How To Locate And Choose A Qualified Practitioner

Researching Potential Therapists

Start by searching for licensed psychodrama therapists in your area. Look for professionals with credentials and training in psychodrama, as well as relevant experience. Websites of professional organizations, such as the American Society of Group Psychotherapy and Psychodrama (ASGPP) or the International Association for Group Psychotherapy and Group Processes (IAGP), can provide lists of certified practitioners.

Evaluating Qualifications

When considering a therapist, review their educational background, training, and certifications. Ensure they have specialized training in psychodrama and are members of recognized professional organizations. This can be a good indicator of their commitment to ongoing professional development and adherence to ethical standards.

Consulting and Interviewing

Schedule an initial consultation with potential therapists to discuss your needs and assess their approach. Ask about their experience with psychodrama, their therapeutic style, and how they handle sensitive issues. It's important to feel comfortable and supported by your therapist, so choose someone who makes you feel at ease.

Checking Reviews and References

Look for reviews or testimonials from other clients to gauge the therapist's effectiveness. If possible, seek recommendations from trusted friends or healthcare providers who may have experience with psychodrama therapists. Positive feedback and referrals can provide additional reassurance.

Further Reading: Recommended Books And Articles On Psychodrama

Books

"Psychodrama: Theory and Practice" by Adam Blatner – This comprehensive book offers an in-depth exploration of psychodrama techniques, theoretical foundations, and practical applications.

"The Handbook of Psychodrama" by Marcia K. Brooks – A detailed guide to the history, principles, and practices of psychodrama, including case studies and exercises.

"Psychodrama: A Comprehensive Guide" by Jonathan Fox – An accessible introduction to psychodrama, with practical advice and exercises for both therapists and clients.

Articles

"The Effectiveness of Psychodrama in Treating Trauma" – An article exploring research findings on the benefits of psychodrama for individuals dealing with trauma.

"Role of Spontaneity in Psychodrama" – This piece discusses how spontaneity enhances the therapeutic process in psychodrama sessions.

"Integrating Psychodrama with Other Therapeutic Approaches" – An article on how psychodrama can be combined with other therapeutic methods for a more holistic treatment approach.

Training and Certification: Information on Training Programs and Certification for Psychodrama Therapists

Training Programs

Psychodrama training programs typically include coursework in psychodrama theory, techniques, and supervision. These programs are often offered by professional organizations and academic institutions. They may also include experiential components where trainees participate in psychodrama sessions.

Certification

Certification in psychodrama is usually awarded by professional bodies such as the American Board of Examiners in Psychodrama, Sociometry, and Group Psychotherapy (ABE). Certification generally requires completion of a training program, supervised practice, and passing a certification exam. Certified practitioners have demonstrated a high level of competence and adherence to professional standards.

Continuing Education

Psychodrama therapists are encouraged to pursue ongoing education to stay current with developments in the field. Many organizations offer workshops, conferences, and seminars on advanced psychodrama techniques and related topics.

Support Groups And Networks: Connecting With Communities And Networks For Support And Further Learning

Local Support Groups

Many communities have support groups for individuals interested in psychodrama or those currently in therapy. These groups offer a space to share experiences, learn from others, and receive support. Check local mental health organizations or community centers for information about such groups.

Professional Networks

Joining professional networks or associations related to psychodrama can provide valuable opportunities for learning and networking. Organizations like ASGPP or IAGP often host events, provide resources and facilitate connections with other professionals in the field.

Online Forums and Communities

Online forums and social media groups dedicated to psychodrama can be useful for connecting with others who share your interests. These platforms can offer additional resources, advice, and support from a global community of psychodrama enthusiasts and practitioners.

Workshops and Conferences

Attending workshops and conferences focused on psychodrama can enhance your understanding and practice of the technique. These events often feature presentations by leading experts, hands-on training, and opportunities to network with other professionals and participants.